LEADERSHIP THAT WORKS

A Resource Guide for First Time Leaders

By: Valdemar A. Hill, Jr., Ph.D.

LEADERSHIP THAT WORKS:

A RESOURCE GUIDE FOR FIRST TIME LEADERS

VALDEMAR A. HILL, JR. PH.D.

Copyright (c) 2015 by Valdemar A. Hill, Jr., Ph.D.

All rights reserved.

No part of this publication may be reproduced, stored in a retrieval system, or transmitted in any form or by any means, electronic, mechanical, photocopying, recording, scanning, or otherwise, except as permitted under Section 107 or 108 of the 1976 United States Copyright Act, without prior written permission.

Printed in the United States of America.

ISBN-13: 978-1514678718

ISBN-10: 1514678713

Library of Congress Cataloging-in-Publication Data

Hill, Jr., Valdemar A.

Leadership that Works: A Resource Guide for First Time Leaders/Valdemar A. Hill, Jr.

First Edition

TO GOD BE THE GLORY, GREAT THINGS HE HAS DONE!

Table of Contents

Dedication		x
Acknowledgments		xi
Introduction		xii
Preface		xiv
Chapter 1	Personal Attributes and Professional Ethics	1
	• Respect	
	• Integrity	
	• Professionalism	
	• Work ethics	
	• Responsibility to self	
	• Responsibility to employee	
Chapter 2	The Role and Functions of the Leader	14
	• The Role of the Leader	
	o Coach	
	o Mentor	
	o Advocate	
	• The Functions of Leadership	17

- Planning
- Organizing
- Leading
- Controlling

| Chapter 3 | Building Communication Skills | 40 |

- The Purpose of Communication
- The Steps in the Communication Process

| Chapter 4 | How to get Employees Motivated | 50 |

- Motivation through example setting
- Recognizing employee type
- Non-monetary incentives

| Chapter 5 | Leading and Motivating an Intergenerational Staff | 61 |

- Generations Time Frame
- Root Causes of Conflict
- Communications within Generations
- Intergenerational Best Practices

Chapter 6	Team Building	69

- Team Chemistry
- Building Trust
- Goal Setting

Chapter 7	Dealing with Team Conflict	82

- Interpersonal Relation Skill Building
- Introspection – Self Analysis
- Building Communication Skills
- Sensitivity to Employee Needs

Chapter 8	Employee Performance Evaluation	95

- Purpose and Objective of a Performance Evaluation Program
- Responsibilities of: HR Department; Leader; Reviewing Official and; Employee
- Traits to be Evaluated
- Pitfalls to avoid in Making Performance Evaluations

- Conducting the Performance Review

Chapter 9   Progressive Discipline: The Dreaded Duty   103

Chapter 10 How to Deal With Disgruntled Employees   114
- Getting to the Root of the Problem
- A Prescription for Turning Around the Disgruntled Employee

Chapter 11 Dealing with Unions   124
- Recognition
- Union Security
- Management Rights
- Discipline and Discharge
- Grievance and Arbitration Procedures
- Seniority
- Reduction and Restoration of Forces

- Hours of Work and Overtime
- Rates of Pay and Classifications
- No Strikes or Lockouts

Conclusion	135
References	136
About the Author	139

Dedication

In loving memory of my father, Valdemar A. Hill, Sr. (1914–1976), who always encouraged me to "stay in the learning mode." His pronouncements had a tremendous influence on my life, and helped me to appreciate the importance of education and to stand on valued principles. This book is also dedicated to my loving mother, Florence C. Hill, who recently celebrated her 98th birthday.

Acknowledgments

There have been many individuals who played a very significant role in my life as I pursued my career as a professor, entrepreneur, trainer, negotiator, and consultant. They are far too numerous for me to mention them by name. However, I do want to single out my sister, Kathleen Dyer. She is the consummate professional consultant and has reviewed the transcript of this book and provided valued comments. I also acknowledge my wife, Jennifer Nugent-Hill who gave me the time and space to author this book.

Introduction:

You've just been promoted from your position as a rank and file, regular employee after many years of providing valuable service to your organization. During those years you demonstrated dedication, commitment, and loyalty. You really loved working for your organization and you had been looking forward to this promotion for quite a while.

However, as much as you wanted this promotion, now that it is here, it is with great trepidation that you approach filling this position. You see, you had never been called upon before to lead anyone. Sure, you got along with your fellow employees, maybe even offered them some advice from time to time, but never was required to relate to them as a forma, organizational leader!

A thousand questions flood your mind! How effective will I be leading a group of direct reports? How will they respond to me now that they have to report to me? What about my personality that could jeopardize the creation of a good working relationship? Am I really prepared to take on this responsibility?

As you ponder these and many other questions, you've decided to learn as much as you can about providing leadership that works. You know that it is not going to be easy, nor perfect, but you understand the importance of having some basic, fundamental information concerning this new activity you will be required to engage in.

This book is the first step in obtaining the needed information that will help you in your new endeavor. It will not only provide such immediate information, but can serve as resource guide for you long after you have a few years under your belt as a leader.

Preface:

There is no controversy regarding the importance of leadership in improving productivity in organizations. Leadership provides the oversight necessary to assure that lower level direct reports are performing their responsibilities as required. Leadership is considered the fuel that runs the engine of the organization. If there is not enough fuel or if the fuel is contaminated, the engine cannot perform efficiently.

First time leaders, who often times are promoted up the ranks, must become knowledgeable of the principles of management and be equipped with the necessary tools to be effective in that position. Without these basic ingredients, first time leaders would most likely not achieve their leadership goals.

If I were forced to opine which of the levels of management was more important, I would have to state that of the leader on the first line. We know that top and middle managers are important because they provide the organizational strategies, policies, rules and regulations that set the tone, tenure and direction of the organization. However, the first line leader has the awesome responsibility to assure that work gets done, as required, by the employees. This achievement must be accomplished with effectiveness and efficiency. This is not an easy task.

This book presents the essentials of effective leadership and guides the first time leader, in both the private and public sectors, through the processes they need to become familiar with and how to implement them. It is noted that many books on leadership exclude information on personal attributes and professional ethics. They hardly ever treat these important subjects that are required to help leaders be effective in dealing with their direct reports. Thus, the beginning chapters will treat the intangible elements of effective leadership.

Chapter 1

Personal Attributes and Professional Ethics

Many books on leadership delve right into a discussion on the role and responsibilities of leaders. They hardly ever treat the personal attributes and professional ethics required to help leaders be effective in dealing with their employees. It is important that leaders manifest the following personal attributes as a part of their daily involvement with not only their direct reports, but with all employees. All of these attributes are closely related to each other and often overlap from a definitional perspective. They all deal with adherence to moral and ethical principles; soundness of moral character; and honesty.

Respect: Remember that respect is a "two-way street." That is, it should not only be expected to be forthcoming from direct reports but it should also be given by you. Notwithstanding the position you hold in the organization, you must earn the respect from those who report to you. How often have you heard supervisors demand respect from their direct reports, but treat them with disrespect? Even with all the technical skills that you may possess, this one personal attribute, when missing from your personal arsenal of people skills, can erode all the good that might have been done in the past.

What is so profound about respecting others is the atmosphere of civility that it creates. Clearly, when employees recognize that they are being truly respected, it becomes hard pressed for them to behave in a disrespectful manner. Sometimes it takes a lot to respect people that don't seem to have the capacity to respect themselves and others. But this is a personal attribute that you should aspire to develop and manifest. You will find that, in the long run, a more cordial and meaningful relationship will develop between you and your direct reports. This will have a more positive impact on the work environment leading to enhanced employee performance.

    You are not being asked to be super-human and ignore your own emotions and feelings when you encounter difficult employees; however, you need to understand that emotional maturity and control are preeminent to achieving the level of interpersonal relationships that are necessary to be successful. We will discuss how you can deal with difficult employees in chapter 11.

Integrity: "Say what you mean and mean what you say." This is a quote that typifies integrity. Integrity speaks to a person's character. One's willingness to follow-up on, and keep, one's word. Leaders who lack integrity are ones who do not take their own words seriously. They say things and make promises that they know they cannot keep. Sometimes this behavior is simply a willingness to "take the path of least resistance." For example, in order to get rid of an employee who you consider to be a "bother", you might make an un-achievable promise just to get the employee out of your office. However, the employee, expecting the fulfillment of the promise, soon realizes that it will not be forthcoming. Such employee may eventually hold you in low esteem, considering you as a person that lacks integrity.

In your pursuit of being a successful leader you will more than likely have bouts with maintaining your integrity. It may not be an easy thing to always maintain your integrity, but suffice it to say that it is important that you do. The key is to acknowledge the adverse impact on your reputation and character that can occur when you behave in a manner devoid of integrity.

Professionalism: Too often we only think of people as professionals when they possess high levels of vocational and technical skills, and expertise within their professions. However, there is another dimension to professionalism. A true professional not only has high skill levels and expertise, they also possess a high level of people skills. That is, they know how to balance their know-how with their ability to exert a positive influence in their relationship with others. I often think of the leader who does everything by the book, but has a hard and callous demeanor when applying the rules and regulations of the organization. Notwithstanding their "professionalism" they do not behave very "professional".

A true professional treats people with dignity; does not consider them to be inferior, dumb, or in any way not worthy of their time or expertise. Leaders that have high levels of technical competence and are credentialed, must be careful not to demonstrate an attitude of superiority to their direct reports. Remember some of your employees may not have the same level of competency as you. That is no reason to make them feel inadequate and not useful.

What is needed in those instances is to help the employee achieve higher levels of competency. These are teachable moments that you can use to make a difference; not only in regard to better job performance but in the work relationship as well.

Work Ethics: Even though it is difficult to find a universal definition of work ethics that is acceptable to everyone, it is generally agreed that it has to do with behaviors that shape the moral character of the worker. Employee work habits, values and attitudes are what are reflected in the workplace and are then considered as the "work ethic". The overarching question is "what work ethic does management wants to see manifested in the workplace?" If the work ethic that is currently manifested is unacceptable to management, it must then embark on a course of action that is designed to change it. Essentially, this means developing dis-incentives to dissuade employees from continuing to manifest those behaviors and developing incentives to encourage them to manifest the desired behaviors. You can play a critical and very meaningful role in this endeavor by modeling the desired behaviors for your employees to emulate.

For example, if you want your employees to come to work on time, you come to work on time. This is easier for first-line leaders to do in that they do not typically have to attend pre-office hour business meetings as may higher level managers. Leaders must model the appropriate attitudes, temperament, emotional control, and sense of fair play in the workplace.

When these behaviors are not displayed by your employees it is important for you to have a conversation with them concerning how these behaviors are not conducive to their personal growth and development on the job. Expound on how good work ethics help employees achieve, not only work related goals, but personal goals as well.

Responsibility to self: So, you may ask what does responsibility to self has to do with leader effectiveness. In my many discussions with leaders over the years, I have found that those who saw a need for personal growth and development and invested in themselves to achieve such growth, tended to be more prone to develop positive working relationships. You have a responsibility to be the best you can be. When you demonstrate that behavior among your employees, there is a tendency for them to have a positive perception of you not only as a leader but as a person.

You should never underestimate how your personal demeanor impacts the relationship you develop with your direct reports. They are constantly looking at you; assessing your behaviors and attitudes, and forming opinions about you that may or may not be complimentary. There are leaders that pay no regard, whatsoever, to the impact they are having on their direct reports. Typically these are autocratic type leaders who are only concerned about "bossing" their employees.

When you acknowledge the importance of self-responsibility, you will behave in a manner that engenders the kind of relationships that are instrumental in achieving organizational goals.

Responsibility to employees: Finally, having a sense of responsibility to employees helps in seeking out ways in which you can not only help them achieve job objectives but personal goals as well. When this type of relationship is established with your employees they tend to be more responsive to your directives.

This responsibility manifests itself when you serve your employees. That is, when you understand that in order to have a positive influence on your direct reports you must serve and support them. Servant leadership is one of the most recent theories of leadership and unfortunately has not yet inundated corporate America. There should be a constant search to find out what the legitimate organizational needs of your employees are and then attempt to satisfy those needs. You must provide the resources that are required for your employees to do a satisfactory job.

At the first level of leadership it is acknowledged that you may not always have the authority to directly respond and meet all employees' needs. But you certainly have a responsibility to the employee to listen to their concerns and determine whether or not they are merited. Merited concerns can be supported by you by taking them to higher levels of management for consideration. You should "go to bat" for your employees who demonstrate thoughtfulness and a willingness to help solve organizational problems.

When employees present work-related concerns, some leaders have a tendency to brand them as "problem employees" and "trouble makers". When this happens leaders negate a wonderful opportunity to learn what is truly happening in their respective area of responsibility, and, thus, are not positioned to take positive action. Leaders, should, instead, create an atmosphere and environment that is non-threatening and conducive to employees wanting to come to work and produce their best efforts while they are there.

Chapter 2

The Role and Functions of the Leader

The Role of the Leader

A key element to effective leadership is the creation of positive working relationships. You have a responsibility to encourage, support, and help your employees become motivated. A more current role of the leader is that of coaching. In this role you will help the employee set appropriate job goals and work with them in identifying the kinds of job actions and time lines necessary for achieving those goals. This typically happens at the beginning of the organizational year and is used in monitoring the performance of your employees during the rest of the year. It also serves as the basis for performance evaluation. More on that in chapter 8.

The purpose of coaching is to help your employees discover career goals, training needs, and to assess their strengths and challenges they face within the organization. You, as coach, facilitate the movement of the employee along a prescribed path associated with the job duties that allows them to become more informed and tuned in to their purpose within the organization. In this regard, you help the employee understand the intricacies of the organization.

Another role you can play is that of mentor. While coaching and mentoring utilize the same skill sets, coaching is considered to be more of a short-term, job-based activity, while mentoring is concerned with long-term relationships. Mentoring can take place at any time and may be informal in nature where the mentee receives advice, guidance and support as they navigate through the complexities of the organization. However, more than that, mentoring encompasses activities designed to help the mentee grow both personally and professionally.

You can also serve as an advocate for the organization. A problem encountered, at times, with being an advocate for the organization by first time leaders is that they may not have enough organizational experience as a leader. As a result, there may not be enough familiarity with the nuances of the organization to effectively advocate on its behalf. However, this can be remedied by learning as much as you can about the policies, procedures, regulations, organizational culture, pecking order, etc.

You must become knowledgeable about the organization so that you can represent the organization to your employees. Remember, employees view the organization through the "eyes" of the leader. Whatever you represent to them will be considered as "how the organization works". So, as an advocate for the organization, you must present the organization in a positive light to your employees.

Through all this, your underlying role is to assure that your employees are adequately prepared to perform their duties and responsibilities in an efficient and effective manner.

Functions of Leadership

Leaders on lower levels of the organization perform the same functions as those at higher levels. These functions are planning, organizing, leading and controlling resources. However, on the higher levels of the organization's hierarchy a greater focus is placed on the planning and organizing functions, whereas, leading and controlling are the focus of lower level leaders.

Planning: It is amazing that so many supervisors engage in their day-to-day activities without benefit of a plan. A plan is simply a method worked out in advance to guide the accomplishment of an objective. It is the function that involves setting goals and deciding how those goals will be achieved. For leaders it could be as simple as deciding what method they will use to achieve the day's tasks, assignments, etc. What is often seen in the workplace is the leader performing non-leadership tasks that should rightfully be done by their direct reports. The claim usually is that they are "short-staffed". However, if you would take the time to plan the work of your direct reports and monitor their performance, you may find a resultant increase in productivity with the same size workforce that is under your leadership.

Levels of Plans:

Strategic Planning:

Strategic Planning is an organization's process of defining its strategy, or direction, and making decisions pertaining to the allocation of its resources in order to pursue the strategy, including the use of its capital and people.

Tactical Planning:

Tactical Planning is a systematic determination and scheduling of the immediate or short-term activities required in achieving the objectives of strategic planning.

Operational Planning:

An operational plan is an annual work plan. It describes short-term business strategies; it explains how a strategic plan will be put into operation (or what portion of a strategic plan will be addressed) during a given operational period, i.e. fiscal year. An operational plan is the basis for and justification of an annual operating budget request. Therefore, a strategic plan that has a five-year lifetime would drive five operational plans funded by five operating budgets.

Steps in the Planning Process:

- Being aware of opportunities
- Setting objectives/goals
- Considering planning premises
- Identifying alternatives
- Comparing alternatives
- Choosing an alternative(s)
- Implementing decision

As you begin the planning process you should <u>be aware of the opportunities</u> that present themselves in the organization. This means having a clear understanding of the internal dynamics that take place. i.e., the hiring of new senior level managers and their disposition toward organizational growth; planned re-organization of functional areas and the attendant impact on job performance, etc. All of these are factors that you should take into consideration as you plan for the day-to-day activities of your direct reports.

<u>The setting of goals and objectives should be a collaborative</u> effort between you and your employees. The importance of including employees in the goal and objective setting function is that it provides the employees an opportunity to gain a more meaningful

insight to the requirements of the job. It allows for "buy-in" by the employees pertaining to what is expected of them concerning job performance. It also provides the basis for on-going performance evaluation, as objectives are met leading up to the formal annual evaluation.

The planning premises are the inevitable obstacles that will present themselves during the day-to-day activities that could prove to be distractions from achieving the objectives of the plan. These obstacles can be unanticipated events, human error, adverse economic impacts, etc. You should consider the possibilities of these things occurring as you mobilize your direct reports to achieve stated goals and objectives.

Further, you need to constantly seek out <u>alternative methods</u> of achieving your goals and objectives as you encounter these obstacles. You need to compare the alternatives to determine the more feasible methods to help you achieve, and ultimately decide on the alternative(s) that will be of most benefit to the organization.

A crucial mistake made by some leaders is the failure to <u>implement the decided upon alternative.</u> Some reasons offered for non-implementation are: I don't have the staff to do it; it will take too long to implement and I just don't have the time; I don't know how well it will be received by senior management. Quite frankly, these are the kinds of concerns that you should consider and address during the time you are reviewing the alternative methods of achieving your goals. The ultimate decision should reflect the findings of the discussions on alternative methods.

Organizing: Organizing includes the identification and classification of required activities, the grouping of activities into major functional areas necessary to attain objectives, the assignment of each grouping to a leader with authority necessary to manage it, and the provision for horizontal and vertical coordination. Be sure you are familiar with this process and the means by which it may be implemented.

The logic of organizing:

1. It establishes departmental objectives
2. It formulates supporting objectives, polices and plans
3. It identifies and classifies activities necessary to accomplish these objectives
4. It groups these activities around the available human and material resources
5. It delegates necessary authority to the head of each group required to perform the activities
6. It ties the groups together horizontally and vertically, through authority relationships and information flows.

What is often called organizing is really re-organizing. The fact is, the organizational structure is already in place. However, you can re-organize your work area to enable better work flow, assure greater access to resources by employees, and enhance communication. This function enables the synchronization and combination of human, physical and financial resources. All three resources are important to get desired results. Therefore, the organizational function is of paramount importance in the achievement of these results. According to *Chester Barnard*, "Organizing is a function by which the concern is able to define the role positions, the jobs related and the co-ordination between authority and responsibility". However, if you are not sure of your scope of authority you may be reluctant to do the re-organizing necessary to achieve greater efficiency.

This re-organization must begin with you doing an assessment of the duties and responsibilities necessary for employees to achieve their job goals. The document that will provide this information is usually the job description. Make sure that job descriptions are up-to-date and reflect what the employees are currently doing. Employees may be required to perform various functions such as, clerical, accounting, sales, marketing, production, IT, customer relations, etc. As organizations grow, it might be discerned that some functions have merged with others, requiring some degree of re-organization.

Organizing includes the identification and classification of required activities, the grouping of activities into major functional areas necessary to attain objectives, the assignment of each grouping to a supervisor with authority necessary to supervisor it (delegation) and the provision for coordination horizontally and vertically. Be sure you are familiar with this process and the means by which it may be implemented.

Organization Structure:

Organization structure is the formal pattern of interactions and coordination designed by management to link the tasks of individuals and groups in achieving organizational goals. It depicts the nature of the organizational relationships as they exist at any point in time and it indicates the authority (or reporting) relationships within the organization as well.

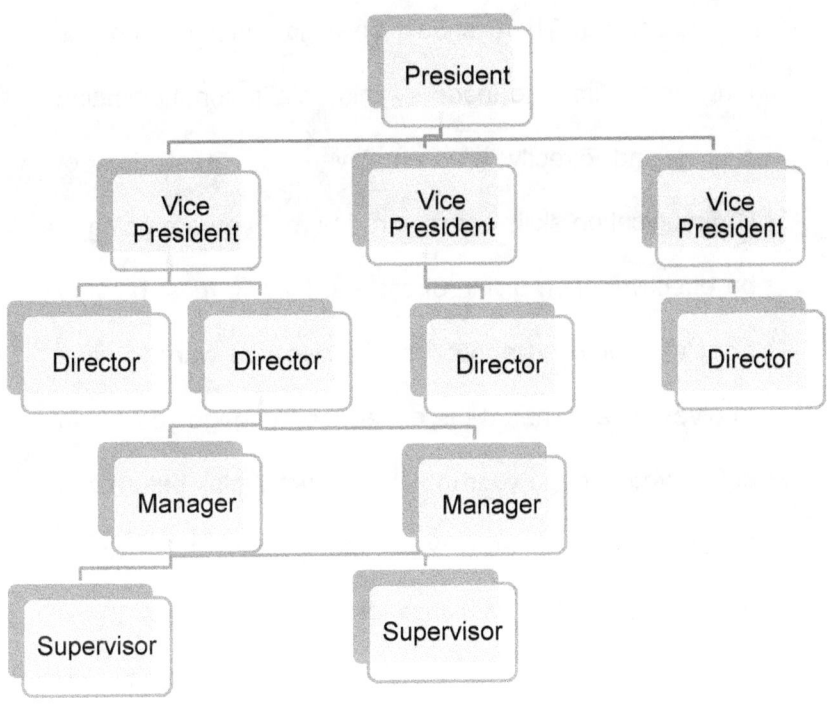

The organiztional structure should be reviewed from time to time to ascertain that the current functional and human relationships are reflected in the structure.

Leading: There should be a greater focus on this function by first line leaders. This entails communicating clearly and directly with employees. A great deal of communication skills are required here if you are going to be effective when giving directives. First, it must be very clear in your mind about the directive you want to give. You've probably heard the old adage, "engage your brain before you engage your mouth". In short, think before you speak. This is an area where many leaders fail to be effective in dealing with their direct reports. They throw caution to the wind and say the first thing that comes to mind without much regard for the resulting impact and employee reaction. In giving directives you should be understandable, polite, concise, and present time tables for task completion.

Leading is influencing employees' behavior through motivation, communication, group dynamics, leadership and discipline.

The purpose of leading is to channel the behavior of employees to accomplish the organization's mission and objectives while simultaneously helping them accomplish their own career objectives.

The leading function gets you directly involved with employee performance, conduct, and accomplishments. It is important to note that you accomplish your objectives through people. If you blame others for your human resource problems, you would have abdicated your responsibilities inherent in the leading function.

There are many types of leader behaviors that have been researched and identified.

Directive leader behavior involves letting direct reports know what is expected of them, providing guidance about work methods, developing work schedules, identifying work evaluation standards, and indicating the basis for outcomes or rewards.

From the very inception of the supervisor/employee relationship you should let the employee know what the desired nature of the relationship is going to be. A clear understanding of the mechanics and operations of job performance should be known by the employees and how their performance will be evaluated.

Supportive leader behavior entails showing concern for the status, well-being, and needs of direct reports; doing small things to make the work more pleasant, and being friendly and approachable. You should develop a mentoring attitude. Also, keep in mind that the more productive and efficient the employee is, the greater the probability that they will achieve the objectives within their area of responsibility.

Participative leader behavior is characterized by consulting with direct reports, encouraging their suggestions, and carefully considering their ideas when making decisions.

As a new leader you should realize that there may be employees under your leadership that have a wealth of experience on the job. These individuals should be sought out and encouraged to give of their opinions in regard to how the job can be done better. One thing that precludes leaders from engaging with direct reports is the belief that they will be thought of as not being knowledgeable about the job. This situation can be avoided if you take the right approach when establishing such engagements.

Achievement-oriented leader behavior involves setting challenging goals, expecting direct reports to perform at their highest level, and conveying a high degree of confidence in them.

Right from the outset, direct reports should be aware that they are working in an environment that is goal oriented. As such, they should be allowed to participate in the goal setting activity at the beginning of the organization's fiscal or calendar year. More specifically, they should be involved in the setting of their own work goals with final determination to be made by you.

Transformational leaders influence employees to perform beyond normal expectations by inspiring them to focus on broader missions that transcend their own immediate self-interests.

This, in large measure, is achieved by your recognition of the importance of a healthy, respectful relationship with your direct reports. These type supervisors have mastered the ability to influence and persuade their employees to operate beyond the mere satisfactory expectations of the requirements of the job.

Servant-Leader behavior encompasses all of the above transformational behaviors but with the intent of establishing relationships that result in the personal, professional and career development of the employee. The servant leader recognizes that the human resource is more valuable than any other organizational resource. As such, these leaders dedicate themselves to helping their direct reports grow in their personal, professional, and career development objectives.

In short, the servant leader serves the employee. This is an attitude that suggests that as each individual employee gets to a place where their potentials are being maximized, the organization benefits exponentially.

Controlling: At the outset, let me say that we are not talking about mind control. As much as we would probably want to control the minds of our employees, that is not the role or function of leaders. Organizationally, controlling means assuring that actual performance is in accordance with standards of performance. It is a system designed to detect when employees are not performing as required and to provide a means of intervention to correct deviations from performance standards. To accomplish this function adequately, there must be standards of performance. These standards should prescribe the manner in which the task, duty, or responsibility is to be carried out including the time period within which they are to be done.

A major problem in some organizations is the lack of performance standards which makes it difficult to effectively evaluate performance. As a result, those evaluations are primarily subjective in nature. More about performance evaluation in chapter 7.

Controlling is the process of regulating organizational activities so that actual performance conforms to expected organizational standards and goals.

The Control Process:

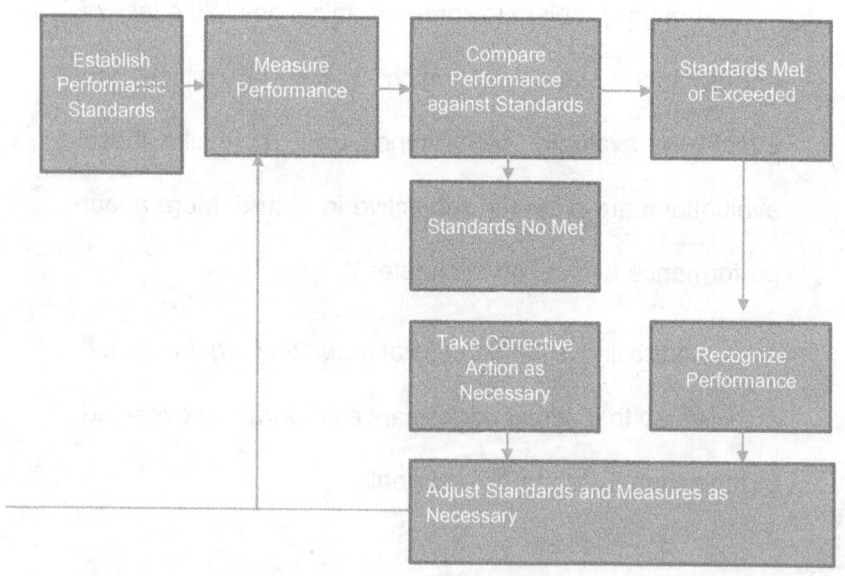

Chapter 3

Building Communication Skills

There is a fundamental difference between communication and conversation. Conversation is usually applied in a social setting with the intent of having a social interaction with others. The purpose is not to persuade, direct or change the perspective (mindset) of someone else. It is a form of informal interaction where individuals "pass the time" engaged in light talks during a social function or relationship.

Communication, on the other hand, has a specific purpose. It is a two-way process where information and meaning is transmitted from one party to another through the use of shared signs and symbols.

There are several steps in the communication process. <u>It begins with having an idea or thought in your mind</u> that you would like to communicate to your direct reports in the way of directives, information, etc. Note, it begins in your mind! This suggests that you must have a clear mental image of the message you want to communicate. It should be thoroughly thought-out before you attempt to communicate. You should also contemplate what the purpose of your communication is.

With this clear mental image you should <u>engage in the process of encoding</u> that message using signs and symbols (words/gestures). Important here is that those words and gestures should have the same meaning for your direct reports as they do for you.

Next is the actual <u>transmission</u> of the encoded message to your direct reports. This is done via an appropriate vehicle (verbal, memo, email, letter, etc.) to convey the message. Learn to use the appropriate vehicle for the type of message you want to communicate. For example, if the message is one of suspension or dismissal, a verbal, face-to-face meeting to discuss the action should be followed up with a formal letter, not a memo or an email.

Many leaders believe that this is the end of the communication process. It is not! As the communicator, you have the responsibility to <u>assure that the message is received.</u> If it is verbal face-to-face, that assurance is obvious. If it is a formal letter, it can be hand-delivered if practical or sent to the employee's last known mailing address return receipt requested.

Once the employee receives the message (letter) they will <u>decode</u> the message by way of interpreting the contents. If there is a misinterpretation, the <u>feedback</u>, which is the last step, may not be as you expected.

Let's look at how this process can unfold. Assume for the moment that you want one of your direct reports to prepare and submit a report to you by the end of the business day. Your manager had indicated to you earlier that it was imperative that she have it on her desk by the next day. You approach Mary, your direct report, around 9:00 a.m. and say, "Mary, you recall that project that you were working on, send me a report for my review." Mary, "OK". Three hours later you call Mary on the phone to inquire about the report and you are told that Mary is out for lunch. You wait for the lunch hour to go by and call for

Mary again at 1:00 p.m. Mary answers the phone and you query, "where is the report that I asked you for this morning?" Mary, "I had no idea that you needed that report right away. I had other items on my agenda to do today, and I was working on them. I didn't think that the report was a priority". You say, "Mary, you must have known that I needed that report today because when we initially talked about the project I told you how important it was". Mary, "I'm sorry, you did not make it clear to me that the report was due today. I will begin preparing the report now, but it can't be ready until tomorrow".

The major error made in the above scenario is that you did not concisely communicate the importance of having the report on your desk by the end of the day. You assumed that Mary should have deduced its importance because of what you said to her at the inception of working on the project. The message was poorly encoded (not sufficiently worded), poorly transmitted (lack of specificity), poorly decoded (misinterpreted), and the feedback was not as intended (non-responsiveness).

As simple as the above scenario may seem, this sort of communication breakdown is common place every day in many organizations.

You need to be mindful that your intended message does not always "get across" to your employees. Here is a fact that conveys the ambiguities of communication and possibilities for misinterpretation: For the 500 most commonly used words in the English language, there are over 14,000 definitions!

Below are some communication pitfalls you want to avoid.

- Errors can occur in all stages of the communication process.
- In the encoding stage, words can be misused, decimal points typed in the wrong places, facts left out, or ambiguous phrases inserted.
- In the transmission stage, a memo gets lost on a cluttered desk, the words on an overhead transparency are too small to read from the back of the room, or words are spoken with inappropriate inflections.
- Communication can be sent (transmitted) through a variety of channels including oral, written, and electronic. Each channel has advantages and disadvantages.
- Oral communication includes face-to-face discussion, telephone conversations, and formal presentations

and speeches and can be ripe for faulty communication.

Advantages are that questions can be asked and answered; feedback is immediate and direct; the receiver can sense the sender's sincerity (or lack thereof); and oral communication is both persuasive and less expensive than written. However, oral communication can also lead to spontaneous, ill-conceived statements (and regret), and there is no permanent record of it.

Written communication includes memos, letters, reports, computer printouts, and other written documents. Advantages to using written messages are that the message can be revised several times; it is a permanent record that can be saved; the message remains the same even if relayed through many people; and the receiver has time to analyze the message.

Disadvantages are that the sender has no control over when, where, or if the message is read; however, some of today's electronic devices provide for the acknowledgment of when a communication is received and opened; the sender does not receive immediate feedback; the receiver may not understand parts of the message; and the message must be longer to contain enough information to answer anticipated questions.

A special category of written communications occurs via electronic media. Computers are used to gather and distribute quantitative data and to "talk" with others via electronic mail (e-mail). Facsimile (fax) machines can transmit messages in seconds through telephone lines all over the world. Other means of electronic communication include teleconferencing, and videoconferencing.

Advantages of electronic communication technology include speed and efficiency in delivering routine messages to large numbers of people across vast geographic areas. It can also reduce time spent traveling to and interacting in group meetings.

Disadvantages include the difficulty of solving complex problems, which require more extended, face-to-face interaction, and the inability to pick up subtle, nonverbal, or inflectional clues about what the communicator is thinking or conveying.

Your communication skills can be improved by enhancing your presentational and persuasion skills. Improving writing skills. Improving language usage and improving nonverbal skills. You can also improve your listening skills; reading skills; and observing skills.

Chapter 4

How to Get Employees Motivated

Motivation: First, understand that you cannot motivate anyone! However, as a leader, you can create an environment within which your employees can become motivated. Motivation is an internal driving force within oneself. It can be described as a passion to accomplish something. It is intrinsic. It is that deep desire inside that compels one to strive to satisfy it. A highly motivated person will go to great lengths to achieve the focus of the motivation. Motivation is that force that drives our behaviors.

A fundamental human resource management question is, "why do people behave the way they do?" The answer lies in motivation. Motives are the "whys" of behavior.

Obviously, you cannot see motives, but you can see the manifestation of motives in the behaviors of individuals. A highly motivated person will go to great lengths to achieve the focus of the motivation.

Motivation revolves around three elements. First, it starts with a need, vision, dream or desire to achieve a perceived worthwhile goal. Secondly, it is predicated upon the person having a "love-to-learn" attitude and who continuously seeks new opportunities. Success is based on learning what works and does not work. Thirdly, the individual must develop the ability to overcome barriers and learn how to bounce back from discouragement or failure. Achievers learn to tolerate the agony of defeat. In any worthwhile endeavor, barriers and failure will be there. Bouncing back requires creative thinking as it is a learning process.

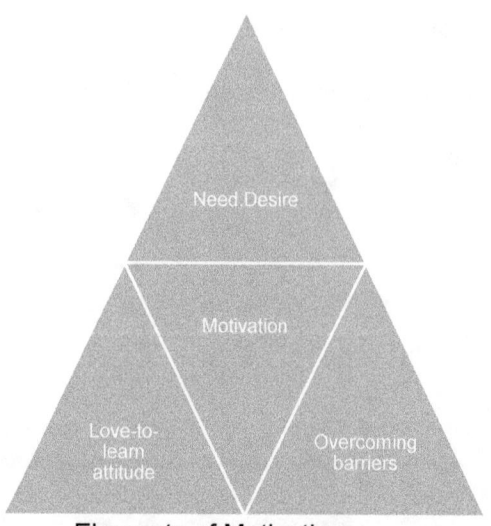

Elements of Motivation

Key to a motivated workforce is your ability to recognize how to help your employees become motivated. You must constantly try to understand what the work-related needs are of your employees. For example, a safe and secure working environment, a fair day's pay for a fair day's work, a pleasant and respectful leader'/employee relationship, etc. If these needs are not attended to, there is a great likelihood that your employees will become frustrated, angry and display counterproductive and unacceptable behaviors.

You, also, must become aware of your own deficiencies as they relate to employees becoming motivated. These deficiencies may include ineffective people skills, ineffective communication skills, and lack of sensitivity to employee needs.

For you to really have a positive influence on your employees it is imperative that you develop effective people skills. These skills include understanding the different personality types that you will encounter in the workplace.

The type A employee is one with the following characteristics: Impatient, has difficulty relaxing, is aggressive, gets angry easily, gets upset over minor things, is competitive and achievement-oriented, has a sense of urgency (interrupts others, becomes frustrated when having to wait in lines) etc. Employees displaying this type of personality are driven by the desire to achieve whatever it is that is set before them. They respond well to challenges and deadlines. Delays, counterproductive conditions, and what they perceive to be unnecessary barriers cause them to display behaviors that are not pleasant within the workplace.

When you discover these personality traits in your employees you should make every effort not to exacerbate the situation by responding in a negative manner; but, rather, adjust your response and attitude that reflect understanding. As you do this, you will create an environment that accommodates their achievement oriented disposition.

The type B employee, on the contrary, shows patience, relaxes easily, is easy-going, mellow, avoids confrontation, and does not get angry easily. They are more creative in nature and take time to ponder and consider how to approach a task and may wait until the last minute of a deadline before taking action. They are more imaginative, pensive, and friendly. They are more "thinkers" than "doers". These employees are apt to be socially oriented rather than goal oriented and can cause you to become frustrated with their lack of concern about meeting deadlines.

The key in both instances is for you to recognize the different personality types and develop an appropriate relationship with the employee that reflects that understanding.

You may be acquainted with the ongoing controversy as to whether or not money is a motivator. That is, would money incentivize employees to perform beyond their current level of achievement? Some employees may even say, "Give me a raise and see how much more I can do". However, if we understand that motivation is internal, an inward force that propels an individual to achieve, then we must realize that external forces, such as money, cannot be a motivator. But we cannot dismiss money that easily, because it has another role to play in the organization. It is what is considered to be a "maintenance" factor. Once employees believe that they are being appropriately compensated, they would be willing to, at least, show up to work. Thus, money, and all other positive needs that are external influences are considered to be elements that would "maintain" the employee in the organization. Therefore, they need to be seriously considered in the employer/employee relationship.

Since these positive external factors are not always present in organizations, or not to the level of expectation by employees, leaders often times have to rely on non-monetary incentives to help employees become motivated. For example, helping employees understand the need to learn, grow, and develop new skills in order to advance in the organization. Once this understanding is internalized, the employee may recognize the importance of accepting assignments and rise to new challenges offered by new responsibilities.

Additionally, where applicable, leaders can offer flexible hours of work and other flexibilities that can help employees meet some of their personal obligations to family, children, friends, church, sports, hobbies and other activities that place a demand on today's employees.

Another non-monetary incentive is recognition. In today's high paced work environment it is reported that employees consider recognition of their work and efforts as rare and infrequent. As you think about it, what better way to have employees continue to pursue their good work and success than to offer them genuine praise, verbal, written or ideally by a public announcement.

You can also provide opportunities for your employees to contribute to organizational endeavors. You can provide the opportunity for them to be a part of the team; to work closely with managers and management; and to be involved in key decisions. You can provide the opportunity for them to be listened to and to be heard.

Further, you, where possible, can enable employees to work independently. Many employees do not want leaders that micro-manage. They do not want someone constantly watching over them and questioning their every move. Employees like to receive their assignments – preferably with the time frame required for completion – and then have the independence to complete the work given the guidelines and framework you have set.

Chapter 5

Leading and Motivating an Intergenerational Staff

If you have, under your leadership, employees with a wide range of year differences and experience you will have to face some unique challenges. You may find that younger folks don't seem to care much about their work. Whereas, the older employees may resent the inexperience and entitlement attitude younger employees may display.

Below are some definitions of the "generations" that experts have developed, and some tips that may help you bridge the generational gap in your work place.

Traditionalists: Born between 1900 to 1945

Traditionalists are sometimes referred to as the World War II generation. They have worked longer than any of the other generations. Having experienced two world wars and the Great Depression many members of this generation have learned how to live within limited means. They, typically, are loyal, hardworking, financially conservative and faithful to institutions. Many are approaching retirement or are retired and now working part-time jobs.

Baby Boomer: Born between 1946-1964

At the time baby boomers entered the work force, they began to agitate for change and to challenge the status quo. Many of the rights and opportunities now enjoyed by the workforce came about as a result of their efforts and optimism to bring about those changes. Their large numbers created a very competitive atmosphere in the workplace as they vied for limited jobs. They worked hard and were loyal to their employers because they believed that was the way to get ahead. They believe in collaboration and consensus-building leadership.

Generation X: Born between 1965-1977

Generation X is influenced by sweeping social change and are sandwiched in between the optimism of the Baby Boomers and the complexity of global relations. They are self-reliant and not as trusting as the Baby Boomers.

Generation Y: Born between 1978 - 1994

Generation Y, is the most recent phenomenon to enter the labor force since the Baby Boomers. These are young employees who have not yet created a name for themselves and are also called the Millennium Generation.

Generation Y employees have lived in a world of unprecedented economic growth and prosperity. They operate in the world of computerization, wireless access and the wide world web. They are natural collaborators.

This age group has moved into the labor force during a time of major demographic change. One in three is not Caucasian. One in four lives in a single-parent household. Three in four have working mothers. At the same time, companies are facing an aging workforce. Sixty-year-olds are now working beside 20-year-olds. Young college graduates are overseeing employees old enough to be their parents. New job entrants are changing careers faster than employers would like, creating frustration for companies struggling to retain and recruit talented high-performers.

This generation of employees have been exposed and programmed with a host of activities before they could even walk. As a result they are both high-performance and high-maintenance who believe in their own worth.

Don't expect Generation Y employees to respond positively to the traditional autocratic type of management still popular in much of today's workforce. They've grown up questioning even their parents, and now they're questioning their employers. They don't know how to shut up, which can really aggravate the 50-year-old manager who wants the job done now and as directed.

Today's youngest workers do not put their careers first. They are more interested in making their jobs accommodate their family and personal lives. They want jobs with flexibility, telecommuting options and the ability to go part time or leave the workforce temporarily when children are in the picture.

Now you see why some conflict is inevitable. There will be tension between employees from different generations. There is an attitude of dismissiveness between the generations. Older employees, not understanding the attitude of the younger ones, tend to dismiss them. The reverse is also true.

How to bridge the generation gap: Steps to success

Now that you understand more about each generation, you're on your way to bridging the generation gaps in your own work environment. The formula for success involves three steps:

- **Be aware of the differences.** Acknowledge that everyone is different. Your colleagues' unique experiences influence their attitudes toward work.

- **Appreciate the strengths.** Instead of harboring frustration over differences, focus on the positive attributes your co-workers possess.

- **Manage the differences effectively.** Once you've acknowledged the differences and taken time to consider the strengths of your co-workers, find ways to interact with them that will be mutually beneficial.

After all is said and done, don't fall prey to stereotyping. Even though certain behaviors may be characteristic of one generation or another, that doesn't mean that all people in a particular generation will exhibit all of that generation's common characteristics.

Chapter 6

Team Building

In many instances the term "team" is misunderstood. Often you hear leaders referring to their employees as a "team" when, in fact, they are really identifying the group of workers that are under their leadership. The term "team" can be described as "a collectivity of individuals collaborating with each other to achieve organizational goals". Inherent in this definition are a number of components that must be present before we even can begin to talk about a team.

First, a team is a collectivity; that is, it is more than one person, it is a group. Secondly, it is comprised of individuals; these are your employees. Thirdly, there must be a collaborative effort exerted among them; fourth, the purpose of the employees is to achieve organizational goals through this collaborative effort. So, the mere presence of employees in the workplace does not necessarily comprise a team. The transition from a work group to a team is in the collaborative nature of the individuals within the group.

As you look at the performance, behaviors and relationships displayed among the employees, one can quickly ascertain if they are merely looking at just a group of employees, or a team. Employees that come to work, perform their individual duties and responsibilities, and then go home at the end of their work day, do not comprise a team.

The members of a team bring their individual contributions to the entire group. They bring their expertise, skills, knowledge, experiences and overall personality attributes and share them with other members of the team. This collectivity of individuals fuses as a single entity with a singleness of purpose, focusing on organizational goals and strive for effective inter-personal relationships.

These are the components that must come together in order to build a team. It is important that you become aware of the deterrents to effective team building. Once the team has been designed, individuals must make a positive contribution. They must maximize their individual contributions by applying their knowledge, skills, and abilities (KSAs). They must pull their own weight. They must also have a thorough understanding of the purpose or goals that the team has been charged with accomplishing.

If this understanding is not present among the members of the team, they will flounder and fail to achieve the stated objectives. Further, a crucial component is the ability and willingness to get along with other members of the team. Notwithstanding all the other attributes, if members of the team cannot get along with each other, it can become real difficult, if not impossible, to build an effective team. Personality clashes can diminish any hope of building an effective team. Thus, the development of good interpersonal relationships is of the upmost importance for effective team building.

In a study on building effective teams, I had the privilege to observe and interact with a group of employees that were the subject of the study. This was a very small group and one would have imagined that team building would have been an easy thing to accomplish. But for such a small group the dynamics of the intra-and inter-personal relationships were very complex. First, the leader, with a human resource management background, had a very laissez-faire management style. Micro management was not practice and employees were free to perform without close supervision. All of the employees were very knowledgeable and performed their duties satisfactorily. Some exceeded expectations.

However, there were subtle and too subtle episodes of office politics, rumors, and personal (verbal) attacks going on among the group. They had been exposed to a team building seminar before and were familiar with the rudiments of building an effective team. Nevertheless, they still could not gel as a team. Individual employees had their favorites within the group and sometimes these favorites ceased to be favorites because of a "falling out".

The group dynamics was driven by personal dislikes as individuals strived to assert themselves as the most "valued" player within the group in the eyes of the leader, and individuals were played off one against the other. Deep distrust developed within the group but they still managed to "work" with each other on a professional basis. The leader tended to ignore the personal animosities as long as work was being done timely and efficiently.

The conclusion by the leader was that the lack of teamwork was not adversely impacting the performance and the results of the organization; and in fact, it was not a team at all, rather a group of individual performers that did not need to depend on each other to get their work done.

You may encounter a situation such as the one described above. The key is to look for early signs of discontent among the employees in the group and begin to explore what is triggering the behaviors. Have one-on-one discussions with the group in an attempt to quash further deterioration among the group. Then, determine if group sessions are needed. There may be instances, because of the nature of the service or product that is being provided, where teamwork is absolutely required. However, if that is not the case, don't be burdened with trying to make it happen.

Deterrents to Effective Team Building

Rumors and gossip about other team members

Lack of integrity   Poor listening skills

Personal values   Personal dislikes

Dishonesty   Office politics
          Lack of communication

Team Chemistry:

In building effective teams, concentrate on the team's chemistry. Pay close attention to the personality differences and the impact these differences have on team development. Guide your employees on how they can gel their personalities enabling them to get along better with each other. Show your direct reports how to resist the temptation to react, compete, or attack each other because of the personality differences. Help your direct reports in developing a "win-win" attitude as they work with each other.

Building Trust:

As a leader, your team members will want to know if they can trust you. Do they believe that you have their best interest at heart? If they came across information that is potentially damaging to the achievement of the goals, will they share it with you? Do your team members tell you the truth even if it hurts?

Trust is one of the noblest of human emotions. It is also one of the most powerful factors you can cultivate in your work team. Trust begins to erode when employees perceive that you are not **walking your talk**. Sometimes those perceptions reflect reality and sometimes they don't. Lying to your team will obviously break down trust; but sometimes the issues is less *you* than it is the whole organizational culture, and in those cases you may have an even tougher hill to climb.

So, how do you build trust in your team? Remember, trust is built over time; it cannot be fixed with one grand gesture. Stop and place yourself in the shoes of your team. This means getting to know them individually and what their needs are.

During deliberations with team members, ask for feedback and be sure to let them know that such feedback is welcomed, even if you do not agree with it. When implementing a decision or program which will be unpopular, be as transparent as possible about the decision making process. Involve your team members in the decision making process especially when choices are hard. Their participation will help build trust for a difficult choice.

Team Development Model

INCORPORATE

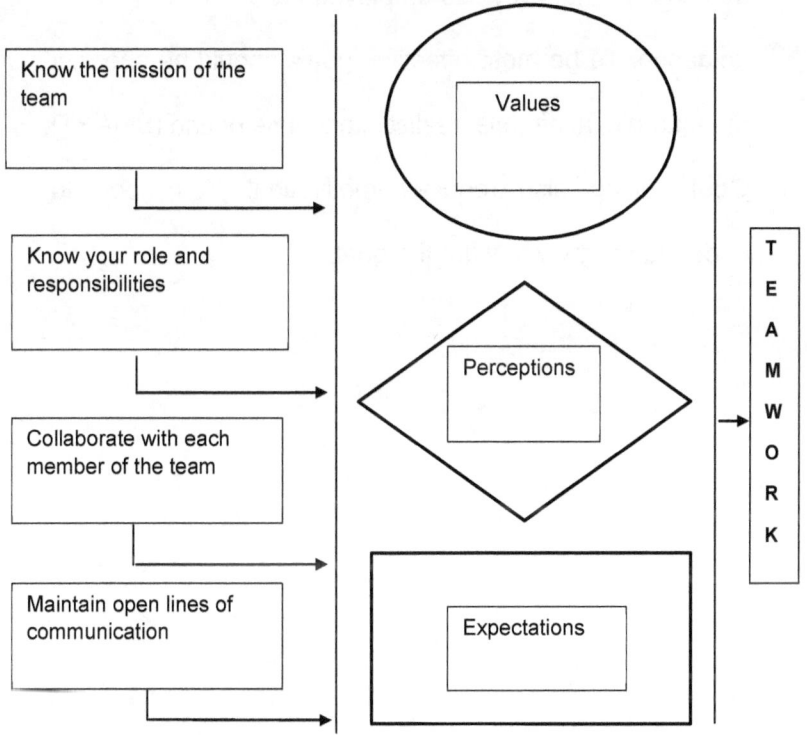

Goal Setting: Goals are an important tool for leaders since goals have the ability to function as a self-regulatory mechanism that provides employees a certain amount of guidance. To be most effective, goals should be specific, measurable, attainable, realistic, and time bound (SMART). Goal setting also requires motivation. You need to understand why you want the goal.

Chapter 7
Dealing with Team Conflict

Successful leaders can effectively manage conflict. This ability is considered a core competency and is required of leaders who want to grow and advance. Unfortunately, it is also one of the most difficult skills a leader can develop.

Conflict can be defined as a serious disagreement over needs or goals among team members.

When dealing with conflict, there are four major questions that should be asked:

1. What are the symptoms of team conflict?
2. What causes team conflict?
3. How do I address team conflict?
4. What tools and aids can I use to help my team deal with conflict quickly and effectively?

You can almost be sure that there is conflict when the following symptoms are manifested:

1. Not completing work on time
2. Gossip
3. Not returning phone calls or emails
4. Passive/aggressive behavior
5. Hostility
6. Hoarding information that should be shared
7. Complaining
8. Finger pointing
9. Verbal abuse
10. Not attending required meetings
11. Filing grievances or lawsuits
12. Absenteeism
13. Physical violence

If you are going to be a successful leader you must help your team become a high-performing one. They must learn to work together to achieve mutual goals. They must recognize that each member is accountable, a team player, and should be committed to achieving team goals. They must learn to communicate well with each other. There must be a balance of team members with the requisite skills and abilities to meet goals. They must learn to share the joy of achievement and the pain of not meeting goals. Help them understand the importance of sharing information with each other and to recognize the success of the group is dependent on each individual. Further, they must understand the roles and responsibilities each has and to respect each other.

The causes of team conflict are varied. For example, if members begin to develop negative attitudes toward other team members because they do not understand their personality type, this could be a source of conflict. Also, if they believe that their Ideas are being attacked or interrupted before they are completely expressed, this will undoubtedly be a source of conflict as well. What if members take sides and refuse to collaborate or compromise and power up on one another? In chapter 5 we listed other ways in which team conflict can occur.

In addressing team conflict you should adopt the following problem solving model: Define the problem → Gather data → Analyze the data → Choose the best solution → Implement the solution.

Below is an example in executing the problem solving model.

Problem: Poor time management (team members not meeting deadlines)

Gather data: How often have deadlines been missed? Which members of the team do not meet their individual targets?

Analyze data: Are team members usually able to meet deadlines? Are they clear about what kind of time management is expected? What kind of mentoring or guidance do I as a supervisor provide to individuals to ensure they meet goals?

Choose solution: Discuss issue with team members. Pledge support in helping them improve their time management skills.

Here are some tools to help you help your team deal with conflict:

- Attack the problem, not the person.
- Focus on what can be done, not on what cannot be done.

- Encourage different viewpoints and honest dialogue.
- Express feelings in a way that does not blame.
- Accept ownership appropriately for all or part of the problem.
- Listen to understand the other person's point of view before giving your own.
- Show respect for the other person's point of view.
- Solve the problem while building the relationship.

Interpersonal Relations Skill Building:

The development of inter-personal relation skills is important in dealing with team conflict. The human experience is built upon the nature of the interpersonal relationships we have with each other. They are necessary for survival in our society. Interpersonal relationships can be thought of as the physical, psychological, social, and cultural dynamics that occur among individuals as they interact with each other in any given environment.

Healthy interpersonal relationships are those that are cooperative, interdependent, supportive, and contribute to our well-being. Unhealthy interpersonal relationships are ones that are dependent, coercive, and non-supportive. This type of relationship can be one of life's greatest sources of stress. At the end of the day, all we really have is each other! You can see then, why it is so important to develop good, healthy interpersonal relationships.

The below elements are necessary in order to build effective inter-personal relation skills. (1) Introspection – self-analysis; and (2) being sensitive to employee needs.

Introspection. When was the last time you took a real good look at yourself? How well do you know yourself? You no doubt have an image of who you are. That is, you have a self-concept of who you are. It consists of your feelings and thoughts about your strengths and weaknesses, your abilities and limitations. Your self-concept develops from at least three sources:

- The image of you that others have and that they have revealed to you
- The comparisons you make between yourself and others, and
- The way you interpret and evaluate your own thoughts and behaviors

Inter-personal relations are a two-way street. For the relations between you and your direct reports to be fruitful, you must be mind-full about how you are impacting them as well. Your attitude, disposition, temperament, and how well you handle the authority position you are in will have a major influence on the nature of the relationship you will have with your direct reports. Consider what about you that might be causing conflict within the team.

When there is team conflict, the first question you should ask is, "what have I done, or said, that might have triggered this conflict?". That's right! Instead of immediately blaming members of the team for the conflict, reflect on your own behaviors that could have possibly caused the conflict. You need to be clear that your actions or non-actions were not the real reason for the conflict before you begin to explore what happened within the team.

In the event that you discover that you were at fault for the conflict, you need to acknowledge that, and find an appropriate way to apologize to the members of the team. By so doing, they will respect you for taking the responsibility and be far more receptive to your leadership role. They will recognize you as being "human" just like they, and subject to err, just like they. This admission alone can be the beginning of a wonderful relationship with the rest of the team.

Relationships are dynamic. They are constantly changing, constantly evolving, and constantly becoming something different. So, after a relationship has been established, it must be maintained. The purposes of relationship maintenance are to keep the relationship intact, retain the semblance of a relationship, prevent the relationship from deteriorating, keep the relationship at its present stage, keep the relationship satisfying and to maintain an appropriate balance between rewards and penalties.

The other element, being sensitive to employees' needs, is just as important and relevant in being a successful leader. Too often leaders overlook the need to assure that employees' (personal and professional) needs are addressed. Depending on the diversity of your organization, employees' needs can traverse the spectrum from cultural, religious and societal to career development, resource needs, and training.

As a result of globalization, you may have to deal with multiple ethnic groups from very different cultures. You may be working in an organization with employees from all over the globe. They may be Japanese, French, Chinese, German, Italian and all sorts of other nationalities. Therefore, it is important to recognize that people from different cultures are different in a variety of ways, including their own world view of looking at things; the way they dress; and the way they express their personalities. This can result in three basic kinds of problems: interpreting their comments and actions, predicting their behavior, and conflicting behavior.

You should learn to develop tolerance and acceptability of cultural and religious differences within the workplace. Tolerance not only maintains productivity and reduce turnover, it can also help companies avoid discrimination lawsuits.

On one hand employers are supposed to be blind to cultural differences but are required to account for them in order to promote harmony in the workplace. To do this, you should minimize the differences between employees and at the same time respect their diverse background and lifestyles.

If you help employees focus on a common goal, that of their company, then they will have less time or reason to dwell on differences between themselves and their colleagues. Building a strong sense of mission and teamwork is one of the best ways to minimize cultural differences.

However, it is never easy to accommodate cultural differences. For instance, if the company gives one group of employees' time off for religious holidays, it may provoke resentment among members of other groups. Understand that sometimes, cultural and religious traditions may also be in direct conflict with business priorities.

Employees may also express the need for resource materials, tools, supplies, etc. to be provided them as they carry out their assignments. It is also not unusual in today's work environment for employees to request child care services and other personal benefits.

Chapter 8

Employee Performance Evaluation

The employee performance evaluation can be a pleasant event if approached strategically. The review process can be productive once employees understand how their contributions affect the organization's vision, values, and objectives.

Putting an effective performance evaluation in place can:

1. Promote consistent, and objective evaluations
2. Ensure that evaluation reviews are done regularly
3. Boost employee and leader participation in the review process

It is important for you to explain the purpose of a performance evaluation system to your employees. It is designed to:

1. Maintain or improve each employee's job satisfaction and morale.
2. Serve as a guide for leaders in planning future training for employees.
3. Assure considered opinion of employee's performance and focus on achievement of assigned duties.
4. Assist in determining and recording special talents, skills, and capabilities.
5. Assist in planning personnel moves and placements.
6. Provide opportunities for employees to discuss job problems and interests with the leader.

7. Assembly data to be used for purposes as wage adjustments, promotions, disciplinary actions and dismissals.

The overall responsibility for the administration of the Performance Evaluation Program rests with the person in charge of the Human Resources functions. This person distributes the proper forms to leaders in a timely manner. Ensures completed forms are returned by a specified date. Reviews forms for completeness. Identifies discrepancies (if any).

Ensures proper safe guarding and filing of completed forms.

You have the responsibility to continuously observe and evaluate the employee's job performance during the course of the evaluation period. Periodic counseling sessions with each employee should be held to discuss job performance. At the end of the evaluation period, a formal performance evaluation form should be completed.

You should not discuss the formal performance evaluation report with the employees prior to having a discussion of the results with your manager. The manager should review for accuracy and objectivity. After you have discussed the results with your employees, if there are unsolved disagreements, the manager should investigate the matter.

Pitfalls to avoid when evaluating performance:

– The evaluation should not be done on just a few isolated performance incidents. It should reflect the over-all performance over the evaluation period. Usually one year.

– Don't be guilty of committing the "Halo" effect. That is, allowing one factor to influence ratings on all other factors. That is the tendency to rate either high or low based on that one factor.

- The "Cluster" tendency is to consider everyone in the work group as above average, average, or below average. Obviously, that would be a disservice to those employees that don't fit into any one of those categories.
- Remember, individuals should be rated, not the job. Looking at, and rating specific performance factors is what is important here.
- The length of employee service should not influence the rating. Rather, the actual performance observed during the specific evaluation period.
- Also note that ratings should not be made purely on the basis of personality traits.

A key activity within the performance evaluation program is the performance review. Remember you have been making observations and having job discussions all during the course of the evaluation year. The evaluation review is the time when you will discuss the results of the overall performance and conclude with an official document that reflects that performance. That document will be filed in the employees' personnel files.

For the review, have a specific agenda in mind. Know what you are going to say, in advance, during each part of the interview. Create a conducive atmosphere for the review. Start the review with a warm greeting and perhaps some very brief small talk to help relax tensions. Be sure that the employee understands exactly how their overall performance ranks. Summarize the overall performance first, and then explain what the rating means.

Unless an employee's performance is unsatisfactory, compliment them on both major and minor strengths as they relate to the job. Avoid saying anything negative until you have reviewed their strengths.

Unless an employee's performance has been truly exceptional, you should provide feedback in areas where they are challenged, or at least suggest room for improvement. When you are reviewing the challenges they are faced with, be as specific as possible. You what to be able to recite dates, times and events as accurately as possible so that there can be no doubts about the occurrences.

After you have discussed these challenges, you should give them an opportunity to air their thoughts. Listen politely until the employee is done. Avoid being argumentative. This is not a debate session. After the employee has represented their thoughts on the matter, let them know that their feedback on your evaluation has not affected your review.

Unless the employee's performance is substantially less than satisfactory, try to end the review on a positive note.

Chapter 9

Progressive Discipline

Progressive discipline is often thought of as the "dreaded duty". That is, many leaders do not want to engage in the necessary confrontation that is required when disciplining employees.

Many companies have gotten into legal troubles because they did not document the discipline that they meted out to their employees. This issue not only has legal ramifications, but also affects the labor-management relationship. Leaders should strive to create an atmosphere and establish a working relationship such that their employees become better at what they do.

The purpose of discipline is to correct undesired behavior; not to punish. Punishment is always negative and personal, a "gotcha" moment; whereas, discipline is impersonal and results driven.

Essentially, there are three categories within which employee problems may occur that may require discipline: (1) Poor performance, (2) Attendance problems, and (3) Misconduct. Employees may have problems in one or all of these categories.

Progressive discipline is a process of gradually applying techniques in an attempt to change unacceptable behavior. Typical steps may include:

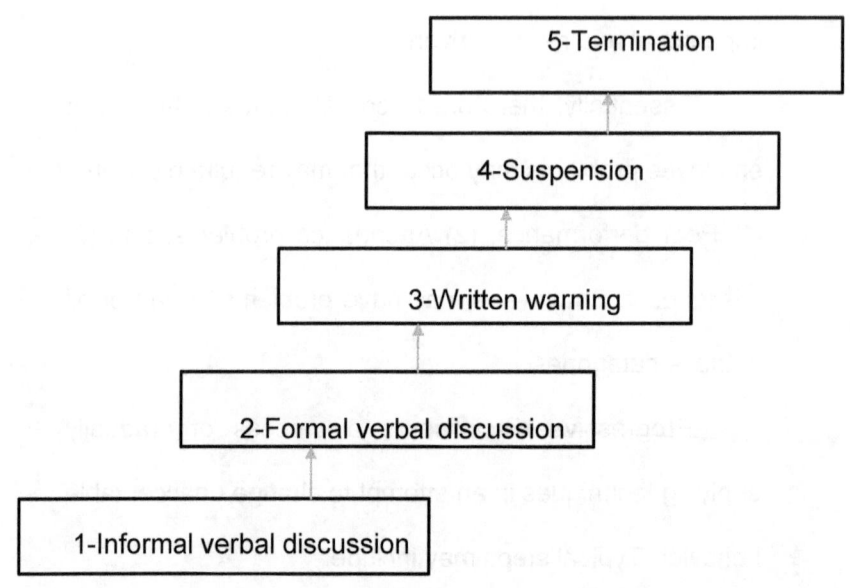

Each step needs to be documented. Even the informal verbal discussion. Notes should be taken that, in fact, such a discussion was held including time, date, what was said by both parties, and what understanding the employee had at the end of the discussion concerning your performance expectations.

Four factors, "FOSA", go into providing for a good system of documenting discipline.

FACTS: Establish what the facts are in the situation

OBJECTIVES: Establish the objectives to be achieved through the disciplinary process.

SOLUTIONS: Provide solutions to correct the undesired behaviors.

ACTIONS: Inform employees of action(s) to be taken if behaviors are not corrected.

FOSA is a systematic approach to documenting all the efforts exerted by you to help your employees overcome the work-related problems they encounter in the workplace. This approach helps you to stay focused on the issues and avoid vague, ambiguous, and meaningless terminologies when describing the problem. It helps you to concentrate on facts, objectives, solutions and actions.

As a result, the employee may recognize the sincerity on your part to help; that you are only interested in what is best for the employee; and that you are willing to spend the time to bring about a practical solution to the problem. Employees may come to realize that the problem is really theirs and not yours.

This approach helps to establish a good atmosphere and a professional working relationship.

You may recall that we said that discipline is always positive and impersonal up to and including termination. Well, you may ask, "How can a termination be positive"?

Certainly it seems like something negative has happened. Well, if you were to look at it from the perspective that an employee, who refused to change behavior, is now free to do whatever they want to do; and further, you have freed up a position in which you can now employ someone who wants to work and manifest appropriate behavior, you will see that it can be a positive action. This seems to me to be a win-win situation.

So, how do you go about preparing for termination? First, determine if the employee actually violated a procedure, rule or directive. This would call for some degree of investigation into the allegation. After being assured of the infraction, determine how grievous it is and if it warrants discipline. Then see if progressive discipline was instituted. If so, review previous disciplinary cases.

Important in this process is to ascertain if the violation was the result of a lack of training or was it performance based. Make sure you are aware of the labor laws of your state or territory and the contractual provisions concerning termination. Finally, ask yourself, "Why must I terminate this employee"?

Now that the decision to terminate has been made, it is important to know what to say during the exit interview. Conduct this interview in private and at the close of business. At this hearing, be succinct and have all the facts that justify the dismissal. Give concrete examples of poor performance. Don't tell the employee, "It's just not working out." Failure to give actual examples could be grounds for a wrong-full discharge grievance or lawsuit.

Tell the employee the effective date of the termination, whether it's today of two weeks later. At the hearing you would tell the employee of the benefits, severance pay, unused vacation time and any other such benefit that they may be entitled to, if any. Limit the conversation to around 10 minutes. It should not be a long debate about the action that you are taking. Don't get into a shouting match with the employee. Treat the employee courteously and do not publicly embarrass them.

If you suspect that the employee might turn violent, arrange to have security personnel standing by.

If the employee being terminated has access to sensitive information or computer files, terminate them immediately and give the two-week notice pay. Change passwords and codes when such an employee is terminated.

Determine, before hand, if there are any legal or contractual obligations you must meet before actually terminating the employee.

After the exit interview, call all remaining staff members together and explain how the vacancy will affect them, the responsibilities that will be shifted and the approximate time when a replacement will be hired.

In handling a disciplinary matter gather all relevant facts. Be clear about the performance shortfall. Determine if the action should be training, advice, counseling or formal disciplinary action. If formal action is required, arrange a disciplinary interview, if the employee is in a union, make sure that a union representative is present. If new facts emerge during the interview review the facts. Consider the gravity of the offense. See what penalties were applied in similar cases in the past. Review the employee's disciplinary record. Determine if there are mitigating circumstances and consider the appropriateness of the proposed discipline.

DECISION TO DISCIPLINE

Flowchart of decision process

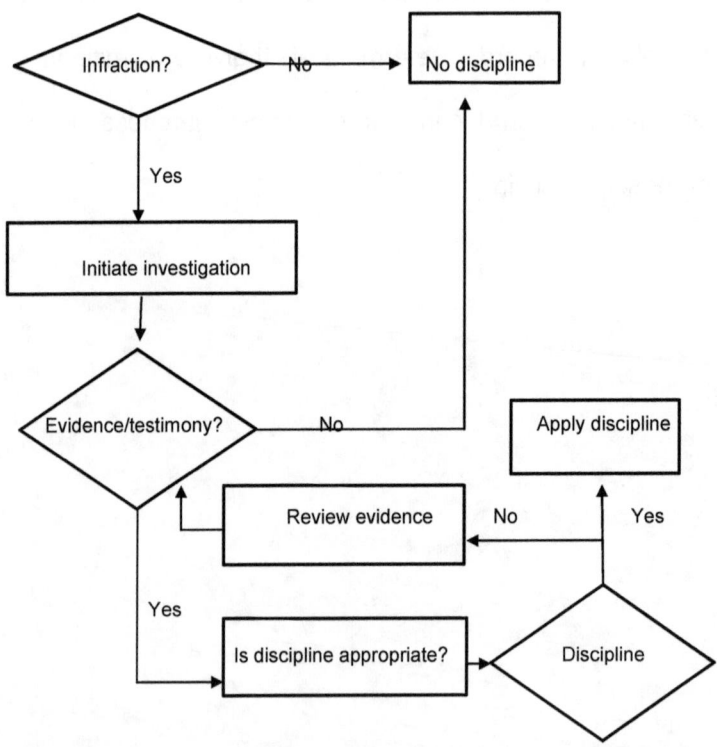

Chapter 10

How to Deal with Disgruntled Employees

How do you know when an employee is disgruntled? A disgruntled employee is one who is dissatisfied with the manner in which events are unfolding within the work environment. Below are some symptoms expressing the dissatisfaction of the disgruntled employee:

Resents authority. When an employee resents authority, this is a clear sign that the employee is disgruntled. Particularly if this type of behavior was not evident before. This symptom may manifest if the employee perceives or believes that management is not concerned about their interests; personal or professional. As a result, you may experience instances where your employees will sabotage administrative directions. Sabotage is hardly ever overt; rather there may be covert attempts to disrupt your efforts to achieve your leadership goals.

You may also see the development of a negative attitude as a sign of a disgruntled employee. This negativity presents itself in employees who always find reasons why something cannot be done. Particularly, as a first time leader with direct reports who have been with the organization for a long time, you may heard retorts like: "We've tried that before and it just doesn't work"; or "We've never had the resources available to get that done".

A more subtle symptom that may suggest your employees are disgruntled is their unwillingness to accept responsibility for their own behaviors. These employees have developed the art of "finger pointing". It's always something, or somebody else's fault. They are never about doing some introspection to determine the motive behind their counterproductive behavior. They will point to bad leadership, lack of resources, poor working environment, uncaring management, hostile fellow employees, etc. Pay close attention to these excuses and help your employees to see and understand why they are not the reasons for their lack of accepting their responsibility for their own behaviors.

How about employees who thrive on manipulating others. Manipulative behavior could very well be another symptom of a disgruntled employee. This type of behavior is often rooted in a feeling that things just aren't "right" with the organization or section in which the employee is working; thus, attempts to "change things around" thorough manipulation. For reasons of their own, they are more prone to manipulate rather than go through the appropriate channels to bring about the change(s) they would like to see happen.

Also look for signs of employees becoming angry and over-aggressive. This is a major overt reaction by employees expressing their sentiments about what they perceive is going on in the organization or with their leaders. The continued demonstration of anger and over-aggressiveness should not be tolerated; whether these expressions are based on reality or not.

Expressing concerns is okay if done in a positive and constructive way designed to correct deficiencies. However, constant negative complaining may be a sign of a disgruntled employee. This is the twin behavior of the employee who is always negative. A complaining attitude can eventually create a hostile work environment if other employees become negatively impacted that results in a reduction of their productivity. Fellow employees who have to work in close proximity of these employees may not want to be around them.

One of the ways in which employees manifest the fact that they are disgruntled is in the abuse of company equipment and supplies. Whether they are field or office machinery, this abuse may be the employees' way of "getting back" on management that they believe has not treated them well. The abuse of equipment and supplies can be a costly venture and you should always be vigilant in discovering these abuses. This type of behavior should almost always warrant some kind of disciplinary intervention.

Keep your eye out for employees who always resist change. We know that change is inevitable whether we want it or not. In order for organizations to grow meaningful change must take place whether it is financial, technological, or cultural. One reason why employees resist change is because they don't have a sense of how it will impact their employment status. It is a good thing, then, before changes are made, to educate your direct reports about the "why", "when" "where" and "how" the change will be made. Be honest about how the changes will affect their employment status and prepare them for it.

Employees that over-react to your directives and who refuse to accept your feedback on their performance could very well be another symptom of being disgruntled. Overreaction could be the manifestation of a behavior in response to a perceived bad relationship between you and your employees. It may also be the result of a lack of understanding of the directive and the dread of receiving feedback that they suspect will not be favorable.

"Talking back", being tactless, non-regard for common courtesy, and being impolite could also be representative of a disgruntled employee. Generally seeming unhappy with just about everything may be a reflection of the symptoms manifested by employees who demonstrate the behaviors described above.

Look for the development of a "you owe me" attitude in your employees. This too may be characteristic of a disgruntled employee. Some employees believe that they are giving far more than they are receiving from the organization they work in. They subsequently develop a sense of "entitlement". You may see the development of a "tit for tat" relationship, and the exacting of benefits in relation to any further required performance. Even though, this perception may not be grounded in reality, you still have the responsibility of verifying if it is so or not.

An insubordinate and untruthful employee is certainly not the model employee and could just be the epitome of a disgruntled one .Insubordination is the refusal to carry out a direct order. It undermines your authority as a leader and challenges your leadership. As long as the directive does not require employees to perform an illegal or immoral act, or one that would put them in harm's way without the appropriate protective gear, or is against their religious persuasion, they have an administrative responsibility to carry it out. They may subsequently challenge the directive through the grievance process.

Telling lies also undermines your efforts to achieve your organizational goals. You have to be able to trust your direct reports in your daily communication with them. Remember, the decisions that you make are partially as a result of the information that you receive from them.

One of the benefits of being an employee is the participation in the various leave programs that an organization may have. Programs such as vacation leave, sick leave, etc. When employees become leave abusers recognize this as a sign of disgruntlement. Leave abuse suggests that the employee does not want to be in the work environment.

As a leader you need to understand that the behaviors described above are often inter-related, and can be overlapping. Some types of behaviors may stem from other behaviors that are prevalent in the life of the employee within the workplace.

We've said a lot about the disgruntled employee, but what can be done to effectively deal with them? Here is a standard approach in dealing with disgruntled employees.

1. Identify the problem in clear, specific and objective terms.
2. Don't assume anything. Gather all the facts and complete a thorough, objective investigation.
3. A careful analysis of the facts is appropriate at this point.
4. Be clear about what you will do if the problem continues to exist.
5. Develop a plan of correction and discuss it with the employee.
6. Complete the documentation; whether it is in the form of a formal report, a note to yourself, or an entry in the employee's personnel file.
7. Follow up and follow through with the implemented plan of correction.

Chapter 11
Dealing with Unions

Many organizations in both the public and private sectors have employees that are members of a labor organization. This chapter is dedicated to those leaders who have to deal with unions and their members.

As a mediator, arbitrator and negotiator over the past thirty years, I have seen the plight of first line leaders and other management personnel as they struggle to deal with the myriad of labor statutes, collective bargaining agreements, and management polices pertaining to the employer/employee relationship. Often times they are not as versed in the provisions of these documents as union leaders and their members are.

It is important that you become familiar with the framework within which labor relations take place.

The National Labor Relations Act of 1935 (NLRA), Section 7, establishes the right of private sector employees to self-organization, to form, join, or assist labor organizations and organize themselves into collective bargaining units to negotiate wages and other working conditions. It also grants rights to protect employers' commercial interests and prevents unfair practices by labor.

Section 8(a)(1) of the NLRA, in a broad sense, prohibits employers from interfering with employees' rights to pursue a labor organization.

The Federal Labor Relations Act of 1978 (FLRA), on the other hand is federal law granting collective bargaining rights for most employees of the federal government of the United States. It is patterned after the National Labor Relations Act with some major exceptions. The FLRA provides that federal employees can only collectively bargain with respect to personnel practices only. They may not negotiate wages, hours, employee benefits, and classification of jobs. Also, the right of federal employees to engage in "concerted action" like workplace strikes, is prohibited. Further, under the FLRA, it is an unfair labor practice for labor unions to call or participate in picketing that interferes with the operation of a federal agency.

It is important for you to know what the labor relations statues are that govern your state or territory.

The collective bargaining agreement (CBA) may consists of several Articles and Sections. Below are some of the more common provisions.

Recognition: This is a provision that calls for the recognition of the Union as the exclusive bargaining representative for all employees within the appropriate bargaining units.

Union Security: In this section the parties agree that, as a condition of employment, the employee shall pay the Union either dues or payment-in-lieu of dues. Payment in lieu of dues apply to those employees who prefer not to be a member of the union. Notwithstanding their non-member status they pay a fee in lieu of dues because they still must be represented by the union in instances where they may file a grievance against management; they also receive all the benefits obtained through the negotiation process.

Management Rights: Whether in the public or private sector, employers have the right to manage their organizations such that they operate at a high level of effectiveness and efficiency. In that regard, they establish standards for hiring, determine qualifications, hiring, promoting, transferring, assigning, retaining, disciplining, suspending, demoting or discharging employees. Further, they determine methods, means and personnel by which their operations are to be conducted. Additionally, they may take such actions as necessary to carry out the mission of the organization in times of emergencies.

Discipline and Discharge: As indicated under management rights, employers have the right to discipline their employees who may be found guilty of some infraction or violation of their rules and regulations, or any other behavior that may subject them to be disciplined.

A fundamental error that some leaders make is to confuse punishment for discipline. Punishment is not discipline and has no place within the workplace. Punishment is always negative and personal; a "gotcha" moment where personalities drive the behavior of the leader. This type of behavior can quickly deteriorate into a non-productive situation that loses focus on the real issue.

Discipline, on the other hand, is designed to correct undesired behavior as described in Chapter 9.

Grievance and Arbitration Procedures: In many collective bargaining agreements, the term "grievance" is defined as a complaint, dispute or controversy between the parties, as to the interpretation, application or compliance with the provisions of the agreement. The procedure encompasses a number of steps (administrative hearings) moving towards arbitration if the dispute is not resolved within the grievance process.

The purpose of the steps is to allow the grievant "due process" by which the complaint is heard. It is designed to give the employee the opportunity to express why they think they should not have been disciplined. As an administrative process you should be doing more listening than talking.

Key to the efficient administration of the grievance process is your adherence to the time limits prescribed in the agreement by which you must respond to the grievance at each step in the process.

Arbitration happens when the parties have not been able to mutually settle the grievance through the grievance process. A third party neutral (arbitrator), mutually selected by the parties, will then hear the grievance and the decision or award will be final and binding on the parties.

Seniority: An important issue for labor organizations is the question of seniority. Seniority is used to determine the relative rights of employees within the bargaining unit. Generally, seniority is defined as the length of time an employee has served in a job or worked for an organization.

In some entities it may be wise to define the different types of seniority that might exist. For example, in a company with multiple branches, or a government entity, there may be companywide seniority or government wide seniority; within the company or government entity, there may be department seniority; and within the job classification, there may be job classification seniority.

The term "Super Seniority" applies to local union officers and shop stewards, who notwithstanding their position on the seniority roster, have seniority in the case of layoffs.

Reduction and Restoration of Forces: In the event of a layoff, seniority plays a major role in determining who is laid off first and who is recalled first. Employees on probation within the affected job classification are typically laid off first with seniority taking precedence. If additional layoffs are necessary, employees within the job classification will be laid off in accordance with their job classification seniority.

An employee who is to be laid off may elect to "bump" (if such an activity is included in the labor contract). Bumping is the process of replacing an employee with less departmental seniority in a job classification of equivalent or lower salary grade, the duties of which the senior employee is able to perform without additional training.

Employees on layoff are recalled in reverse order of the layoff providing they have the ability to perform the required work without additional training.

Hours of Work and Overtime: Provisions regarding hours of work and overtime will most likely be found in every union contract except those of the federal government and some state labor laws.

Under this provision the work day and work week are defined. The required hours of work within the work day and the work week are also determined. This determination establishes when overtime may be applied and paid.

Rates of Pay and Classification: With the exception of federal and some state employees as noted above, rates of pay are negotiated and are subsequently reflected in a pay plan. The plan represents a clustering of job classifications within job grades moving along a continuum referred to as steps. Each step within a job grade represents an increase in pay.

No Strike or Lockout: To preclude a disruption in the business of the company or government, there may be a no strike/lockout provision within the labor contract. Such a provision prohibits labor from engaging in a strike or other concerted effort to withhold their labor in the event of a labor dispute. To address such disputes, the grievance and arbitration procedure is effectuated.

Management also agrees not to lock out (shut the entrance gates to their facilities to prevent employees from reporting to work) when such disputes occur.

Conclusion

The author recognizes that many first time leaders come up through the ranks and in many instances don't have the requisite skills and experiences to be effective in their new assignments. They may have been outstanding performers as a rank and file employee, but nothing that they would have done in those positions would have qualified them to be an effective leader. Now they are called upon to perform leadership functions of planning, organizing, leading and controlling operations and people; functions they were not required to perform before.

This book serves as another resource at their disposal to help them in carrying out this new, awesome responsibility and precludes them from engaging in trial and error as they navigate through the leadership waters.

REFERENCES

Bartol, K. M., & Martin, D. C. (1991). *Management*. McGraw-Hill.

Bass, B. M., & Avolio, B. J. (1994). *Improving organizational effectiveness through transformational leadership*. Thousand Oaks, CA:Sage Publications Inc.

Bennis, W. (1984). The 4 competencies of leadership. *Training and Development Journal,38*(8),14-19.

Bennis, W., & Nanus, B.(1985). *Leaders:The strategies for taking charge*. New York: Harper Collins.

Burns, J. M. (1978). *Leadership*. New York: Harper & Row Publishers,Inc.

Covey, S. R. (1992). *Principle-centered leadership*. New York: Simon & Schuster.

Dichter, E. (1971). *Motivating human behavior*. McGraw-Hill.

Dunham, R. B. (1984). *Organizational behavior: People & processes in management*. Irwin.

Fairholm, G. W. (1991). *Values leadership: Toward a new philosophy of leadership.* New York: Praeger.

Fiedler, F. E. (1967). *A theory of leadership effectiveness.* New York: McGraw-Hill.

Greenleaf, R. K. (1970). *Servant as a leader.* Indiana: The Robert K. Greenleaf Center for Servant-Leadership.

Greenleaf, R. K. (1977). *Servant leadership: A journal into the nature of legitimate power & greatness.* New York: Paulist Press.

Greenleaf, R. K. (1998). *The power of servant leadership.* San Francisco, CA: Berrett-Koehler.

Herbert, T. T. (1976). *Dimensions of organizational behavior.* Mcmillan Publishing Co.

Hunter, J.C. (2004). *The world's most powerful leadership principle: How to become a servant leader.* New York: Crown Business.

Maxwell, J. C. (1998). *The 21 irrefutable laws of leadership.* Thomas Nelson,Inc.

Northouse, P. G. (2004). *Leadership: Theory and practice* (3rd ed.). Thousand Oaks, CA: Sage Publications.

Rost, J. C. (1991). *Leadership for the twenty-first century.* Westport, CT: Greenwood Publishing Group, Inc.

Senge, P. M. (1990). *The leader's new work: Building learning organizations. Sloan Management Review,* 7(23).

Spears, L.C. (1998). *The power of servant leadership.* California: Berrett Koehler.

About Dr. Valdemar A. Hill, Jr.

Dr. Hill was born in the United States Virgin Islands. He has a Bachelor of Arts degree in languages, a Master's degree in Business Administration (MBA) and a Ph.D. in Organization and Management with a specialization in leadership.

Dr. Hill is a retired tenured business professor from the University of the Virgin Islands where he taught both undergraduate and graduate courses for over 20 years.

As a labor arbitrator, he was registered on the panels of the Federal Mediation & Conciliation Service, the American Arbitration Association, and the Virgin Islands Public Employees Relations Board. He is certified as a mediator by the U.S. Department of Justice, the U.S.

District Court of the Virgin Islands, the Superior Court of the Virgin Islands and the Virgin Islands Public Employees Relations Board. Dr. Hill is also certified as a Conflict Manager by the Center for Conflict Dynamics at Eckerd College, St. Petersburg, FL., and is a member of the Institute of Management Consultants USA.

Dr. Hill has served on numerous government boards and commissions in the U.S. Virgin Islands. He is the Vice President of the Virgin Islands Mediation Services, and was the Chairman of the Board of Directors at the Governor Juan F. Luis Hospital and Medical Center.

Dr. Hill is President and CEO of The Hill Group, a leadership development and training consulting company. He has presented numerous seminars and workshops on leadership development and management, and supervisory and employee training. He has authored numerous publications on leadership, management and economics. He is also the author of *Self-Help for Employees: Achieving Success in the Organization Jungle.*

Dr. Hill's passion is to teach the principles of effective management and leadership, and best practices of learning organizations. He acknowledges the spiritual dimension of organizational life and believes in the high calling of teachers to enlighten leaders to lead with compassion and purpose.

www.ingramcontent.com/pod-product-compliance
Lightning Source LLC
Chambersburg PA
CBHW051917170526
45168CB00001B/431